ESL Teaching Id

Grades K-8

Written by Paul and Clare Reid
Illustrated by S&S Learning Materials

ISBN 1-55035-547-3
ESL Teaching Ideas, SSR1-12
Copyright 1998 S&S Learning Materials
Rev. 2002
15 Dairy Avenue
Napanee, Ontario
K7R 1M4
All Rights Reserved * Printed in Canada
A Division of the Solski Group

Published in Canada by:
S&S Learning Materials
15 Dairy Avenue
Napanee, Ontario
K7R 1M4
www.sslearning.com

Published in the United States by:
T4T Learning Materials
5 Columba Drive PMB 175
Niagara Falls, New York
14305
www.t4tlearning.com

Look For Other Language Units

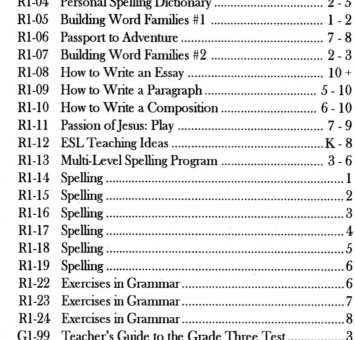

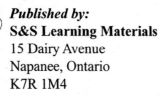

Published by:
S&S Learning Materials
15 Dairy Avenue
Napanee, Ontario
K7R 1M4

Distributed in U.S.A. by:
T4T Learning Materials
5 Columba Drive, Suite 17₅
Niagara Falls, New York
14305

2

SSR1-12

Table of Contents

Objectives

The student will begin to develop basic English speaking skills.

The student will use the Roman alphabet.

The student will write personal information.

The student will be immersed in English through a range of experiences which include oral games, illustration, writing and exploration of his/her environment.

The student will acquire basic vocabulary with respect to themselves, body parts, school, colors, shapes, clothing, weather and seasons.

The student will recognize and respond to a greater variety of words.

The student will use familiar words and some simple grammatical structures.

The student will develop an appreciation for English picture books.

 SSR1-12

Teacher Suggestions

Speak slowly and use simple sentence structures.

Use facial expression and gestures to emphasize meaning.

Remember that a picture is worth a thousand words! This is especially true for new English speakers. Draw or show a picture of what you are discussing to improve the student's comprehension.

If possible, seat ESL students near a peer who speaks the same first language. Having a translator can help a great deal during the new student's adjustment period. New students may go through a silent period.

Label objects around the room. This helps the student begin to make meaningful connections between the spoken word and print.

Increase "wait time" for responses. ESL students need additional time to produce the correct vocabulary and formulate an answer.

Repeat instructions, both orally and in writing. In student writing, be sure to emphasize content over spelling and grammar.

Demonstrate or model new concepts and directions. Ask the student to then show you so that you can check his/her comprehension.

Use concrete materials. Play games which provide repetition of target vocabulary. Practice is needed to achieve fluency.

Involve the ESL student in groups. It is beneficial for them to hear good role models speaking and reading. This also helps to increase the ESL student's self-confidence and vocabulary.

The ESL student needs time and encouragement as he/she moves along the language continuum. Oral skills generally develop quickly while reading and writing skills follow more slowly.

Oral Games

Students learning English as a second language need plenty of opportunities to hear and speak their new language. Provide opportunities to play games which provide repetition and practice of common sentence and question formats. These games provide a good starting point for students and may be played with the pictures provided in Visual Aids, pages 59-72. They may be played with a small group or with individual students.

To begin, show a picture card and name the item on it. Depending on the age and ability of your student(s), repeat this with four to seven cards. Give them a set of matching picture cards and ask them to match each to those you have put down. Repeat the target words as the student matches. Then, holding out your hand, ask the student to return each pair to you, one at a time. This will help you observe if they can recall any of the new vocabulary. Then mix the cards up and put them face-down, on the table. Now you are ready to play *Concentration*. Demonstrate first, by choosing two random cards, turning them over and naming them. Ask "Are they the same?". Say "No" and turn them back down if they do not match. Then have your student take a turn. Many students are familiar with this game or will catch on quickly. When a matching pair is turned over, it is kept by the player whose turn it is, until the end of the game. Most matching sets produce a winner.

When the student is a little more familiar with the target vocabulary, and you want to use a larger number of cards, play the old classic game of *Fish*. Use two sets of matching picture cards. Deal four to each player. In turn, each player asks the next, "Do you have a _____?" and receives the answer "Yes I do" or "No, I don't. Go Fish." You "fish" from the pile of cards left over from the deal. This provides an easy way for the student to learn an appropriate way to ask for something. As in *Concentration*, the player with the most matches is the winner.

Tic Tac Toe is another great game that requires little time to create and provides repetition of the target vocabulary in a fun format. A blank Tic Tac Toe grid is provided on page 73. Choose nine picture cards from the Visual Aids section, pages 59-72, which illustrate the words you wish to practice with the student. Arrange them on the grid. You may wish to cut out five X and five O shapes, or use other markers to cover the pictures. In order to cover a spot, the player must first correctly name the item in that position. Three X's or O's placed horizontally, vertically or diagonally wins the game. If you find that a student is having trouble recalling a particular word, place it in the middle box so that it is repeated more often.

There are four different *Bingo* cards provided to use with the School, Clothing, Getting To Know Me and Weather sections of this unit. Initially, the teacher should show the picture card and name the item while the student looks for it on his/her card. Cover the whole card to win the game. After the student has become more familiar with the key vocabulary, have him/her become the caller for the game. Another variation of this game is *Riddle Bingo*. Instead of naming the item to be found on the Bingo card, the caller gives clues and the players must guess which item is to be covered.

Bibliography

Borden, Louise; **Caps, Hats, Socks and Mittens**. Scholastic, Inc.; 1989

Damon, Laura; **Funny Fingers, Funny Toes**. Troll Associates, 1988

Hoban, Tana; **Circles, triangles and squares**. MacMillan Publishing Co., 1974

Hoban, Tana; **Red, Blue, Yellow Shoe**. Greenwillow Books, 1986

Hoban, Tana; **Shapes, Shapes, Shapes**. Greenwillow Books, 1986

McMillan, Bruce; **One, Two, One Pair**. Scholastic Inc., 1991

Perkins, Al; **The Ear Book**. Random House, 1968

Perkins, Al; **The Nose Book**. Random House, 1970

Serfozo, Mary; **Who Said Red?** Scholastic Inc., 1988

Walton, Rick; **How Many, How Many, How Many**. Candlestick Press, 1993

Getting To Know Me

Introduction to Activities

Begin with oral activities. Choose a small number of pictures from the Visual Aids cards (pages 59-61) and name them, having the student repeat after you. Give him/her duplicate cards to match to the original set. Play a matching game with the pairs of cards, turning them over for a greater challenge. Add to the number of cards you use each day until the student has mastered all of the vocabulary.

Teach songs, chants or fingerplays related to the key vocabulary, such as "Head and Shoulders, Knees and Toes" to provide additional oral practice for the student.

Play "Tic Tac Toe" or "Body Bingo" for a few minutes each day to provide repetition of the key vocabulary. (Provided on pages 9-13) You may wish to use a peer buddy to do this with the ESL student.

Use page 14 to reinforce word recognition describing the head and face.

Use page 15 to reinforce word recognition describing the body. The student should draw the face and hair.

Page 16, "Where do I belong?" should be done together with the student. Note whether or not he/she is able to read each word independently. If not, read it aloud and assist the student with placing the word in the correct column.

Make sufficient copies of page 17, "Family Picture Cards" for the student to color, cut out and glue onto construction paper squares, for greater durability. Use them for oral practice first; i.e. "This is my father. His name is _____." Make a set of the word cards provided on page 18 to use for a matching game.

The final activity in this secton, found on pages 19 and 20 is a booklet for the student to list and illustrate his or her personal information.

Tic/Tac/Toe

 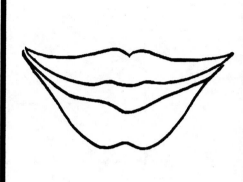 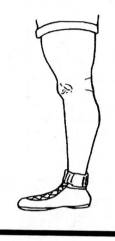

   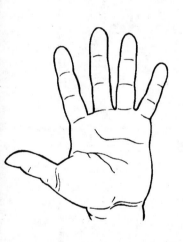

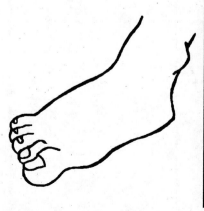 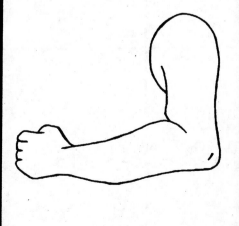 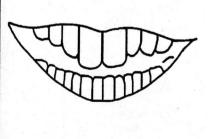

Body Bingo

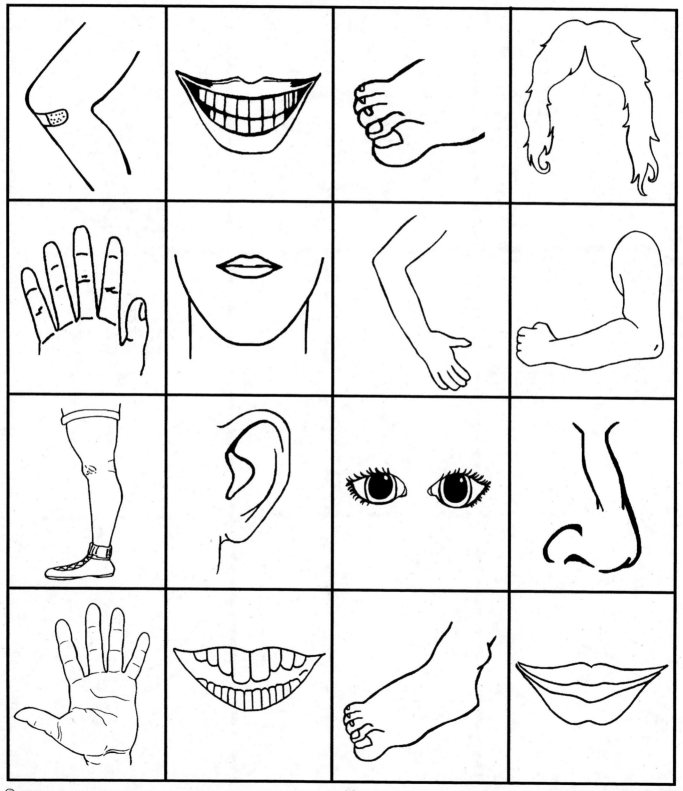

SSR1-12

Body Bingo

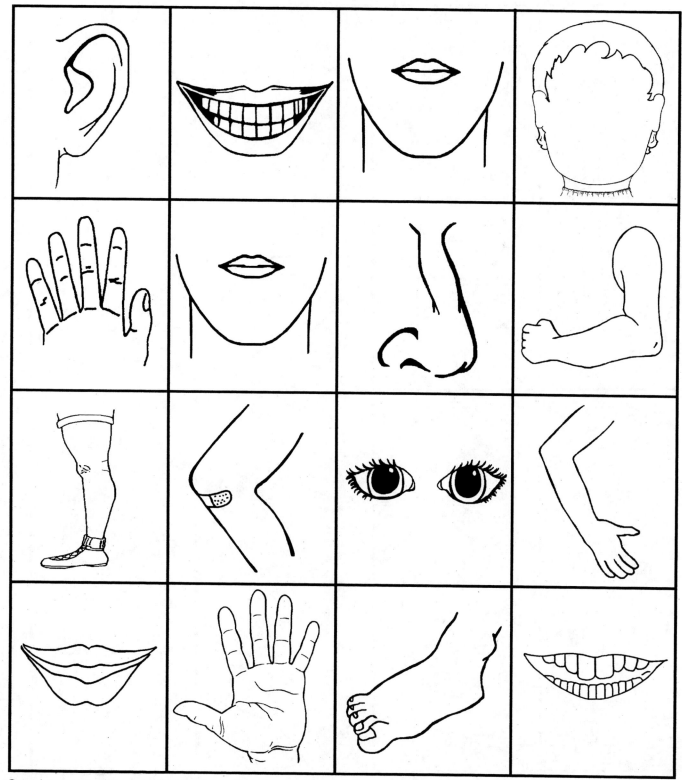

Body Bingo

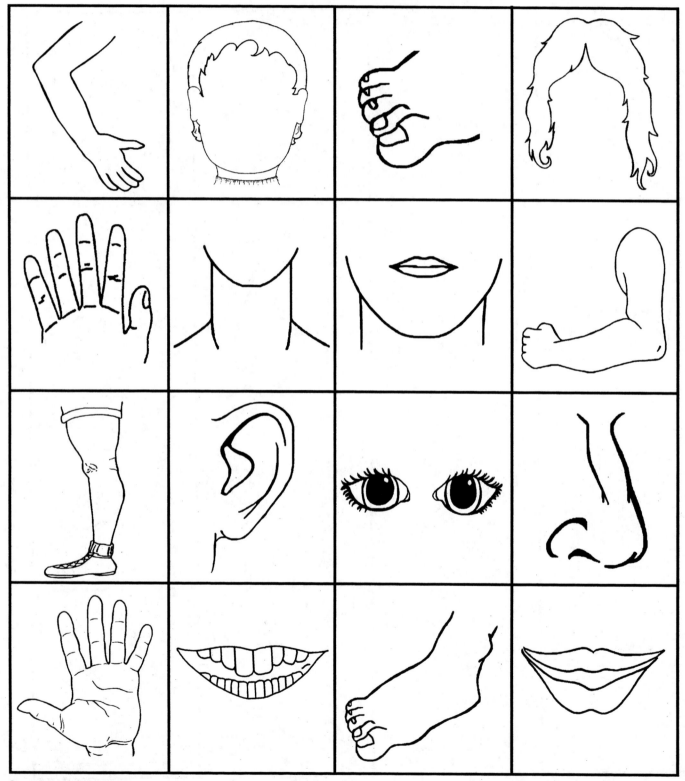

Body Bingo

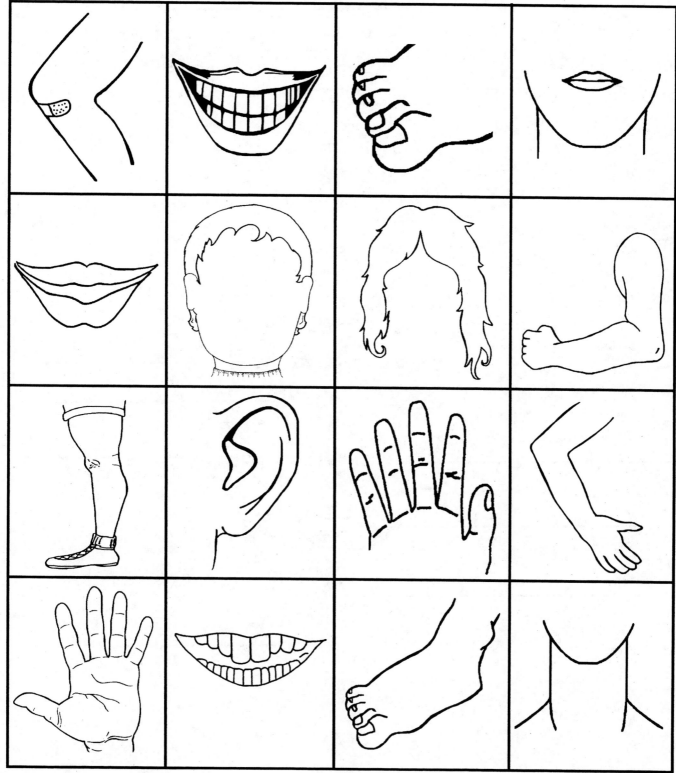

Getting To Know Me

nose	mouth	ear	eye	eyebrow
cheek	chin	hair	teeth	neck

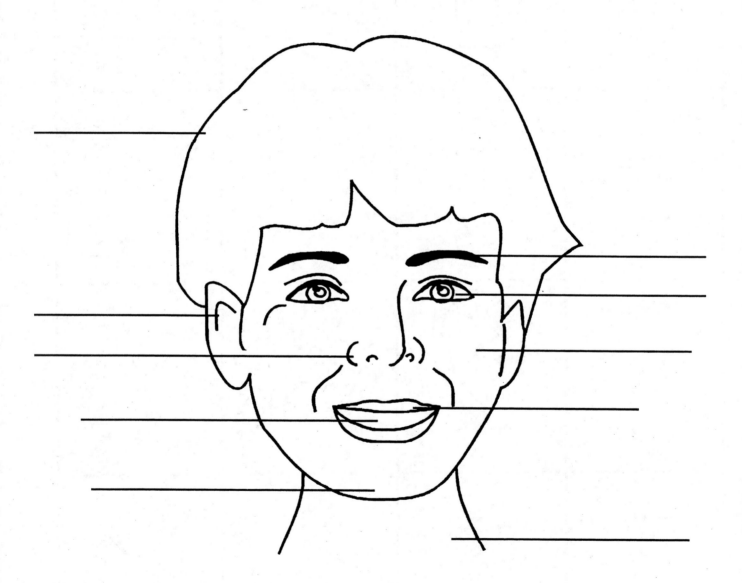

Getting To Know Me

leg	hand	arm	foot	neck
face	elbow	toes	fingers	hair

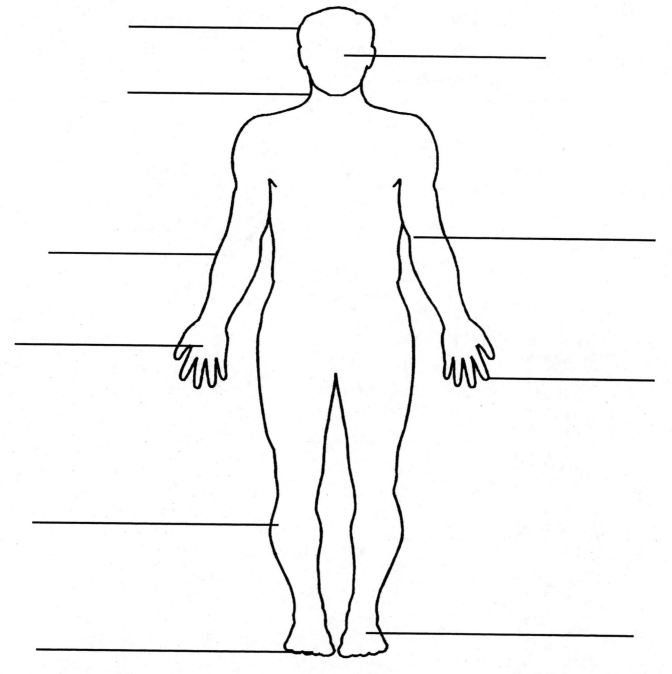

Getting To Know Me

Where do I belong?

cheek	foot	ear	chin	hand
mouth	toes	elbow	hair	eyebrow
nose	neck	eye	arm	teeth
	fingers		leg	

Head   **_Face_**   **_Body_**

_____   _____   _____

_____   _____   _____

                 _____   _____

                 _____   _____

                 _____   _____

                 _____   _____

                                  _____

SSR1-12

Getting To Know Me

Family Picture Cards

Father	Mother
Sister	Brother
Grandfather	Grandmother

17

SSR1-12

Getting To Know Me

Family Picture Cards

Father	Mother
Sister	Brother
Grandfather	Grandmother

Getting To Know Me

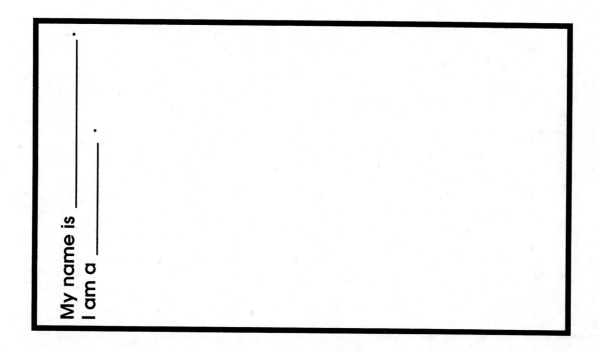

My name is _____ .
I am a _____ .

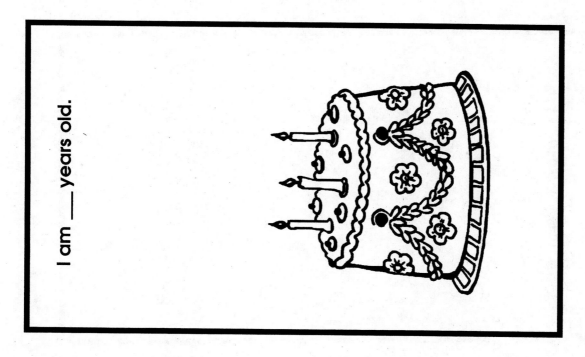

I am ___ years old.

Getting To Know Me

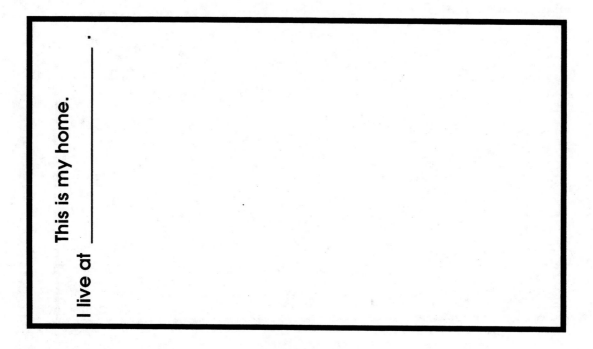

This is my home.

I live at _____ .

This is my family.

Colors and Shapes
Introduction to Activities

Duplicate, color, cut out and mount the set of color cards found on page 22. Begin with oral matching activities. Find objects in the room of the same color to provide additional repetition of the target vocabulary. The student may sort buttons by color, placing them on the appropriate card. Play "Tic Tac Toe", using the color cards.

Teach songs, chants or fingerplays related to the vocabulary, such as "I Can Sing A Rainbow". Read picture books and focus on the colors shown in them.

Begin page 23 with the student. Match the word on each balloon to the appropriate card. The student should then be able to complete the page independently.

Complete page 24 with the student. Point to the picture to illustrate the new words; flowers, stems, leaves and flowerpot. Note whether or not the student recognizes the color words as you point to them.

Page 25, Shape Chart should be introduced orally. Look around the room to find objects that can be classified by shape. Have the student color each shape and mount the chart on construction paper. Display it in the room for reference purposes. Use the shape cards found on page 65 for oral game practice.

The student may then complete page 26 independently, copying the name under each shape.

Read picture books on shapes. Tana Hoban has published several excellent shape books. (See bibliography - page 7)

Use pages 27 and 28 for further reinforcement of color and shape vocabulary.

Have student make a picture by cutting out various shapes and pasting them together. Ask him/her to name each shape orally.

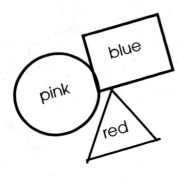

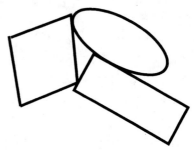

Colors and Shapes

Color Cards

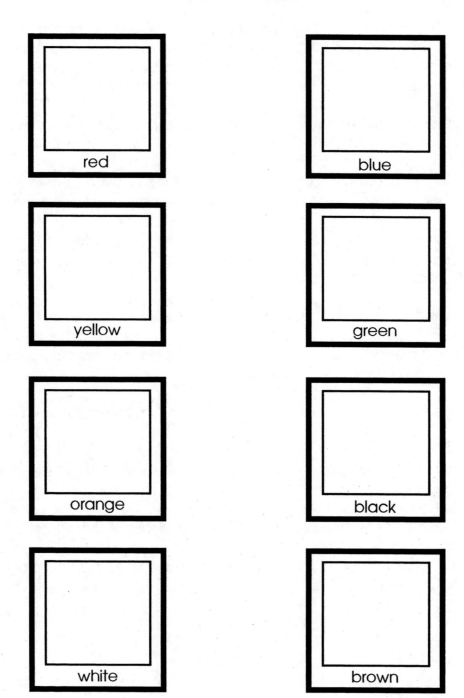

red	blue
yellow	green
orange	black
white	brown

SSR1-12

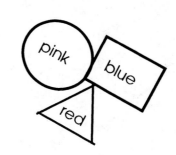

Colors and Shapes

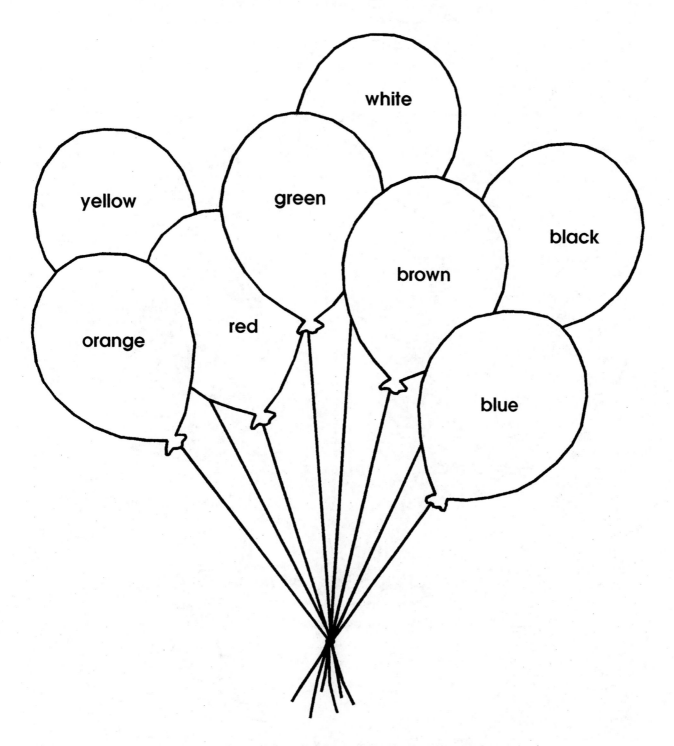

Colors and Shapes

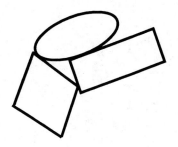

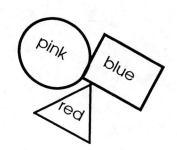

Colors and Shapes

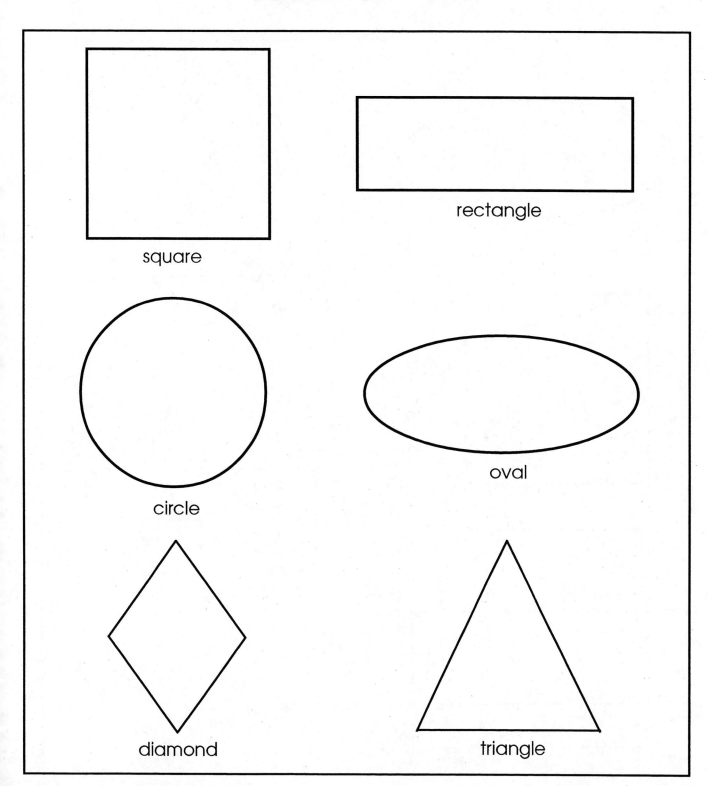

square

rectangle

circle

oval

diamond

triangle

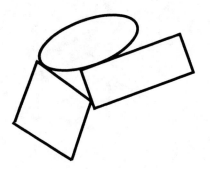

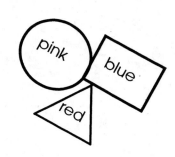

Colors and Shapes

_____

_____

_____

_____

_____

_____

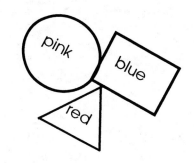

Colors and Shapes

Color the **square red**.

Color the **rectangle orange**.

Color the **oval green**.

Color the **triangle brown**.

Color the **circle yellow**.

Color the **diamond blue**.

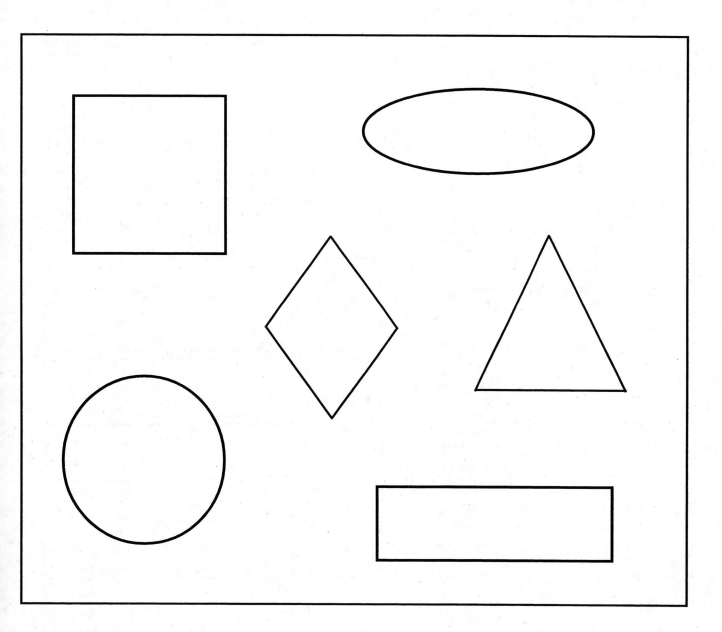

SSR1-12

  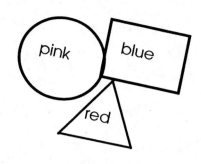

Colors and Shapes

Draw and color **3 red circles**.

Draw and color **2 orange rectangles**.

Draw and color **5 yellow ovals**.

Draw and color **1 blue triangle**.

Draw and color **4 green squares**.

Draw and color **5 black diamonds**.

Draw and color **2 white triangles**.

Draw and color **3 brown squares**.

Draw and color **4 yellow circles**.

Draw and color **1 blue oval**.

SSR1-12

My School

Introduction to Activities

Duplicate, cut out and mount individual pictures of the school items, found in Visual Aids, pages 66-68. Use them for oral practice and matching games.

Four different "School Bingo" cards are provided on pages 30-33. Use these for additional reinforcement of the target vocabulary.

On page 34, the student should first orally name each school item and then label them, using the word bank provided.

Have the student walk around the room with you or a peer and orally identify items found.

Use page 35 to review color words and for additional practice of school vocabulary.

A school wordsearch is provided on page 36. Be sure the student understands how to complete a wordsearch. He/she can then complete it independently. Observe whether or not the student is able to guess the word from the initial letter or appears to be recognizing any of the words by sight.

The final activity in this section is a student book, found on pages 37-38. It is specific to your own school setting. The student may require assistance with spelling and writing the school and teacher's name. He/she will illustrate each page with a picture corresponding to the text. A personal cover page for the booklet may also be assigned.

School Bingo

School Bingo

School Bingo

32

SSR1-12

School Bingo

School Bingo

Label each picture. Use the words from the word bank below.

glue	pencil	crayons	pen	desk
stapler	scissors	marker	paper	computer

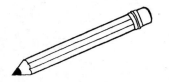
_____

_____

_____

_____

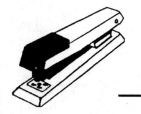
_____

_____

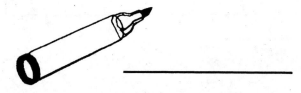
_____

_____

_____

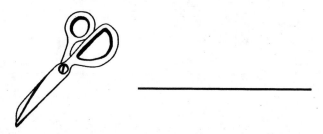
_____

My School

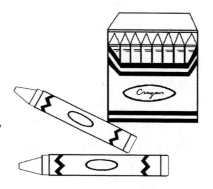

Color the box of crayons different colors.

Color the pencil yellow.

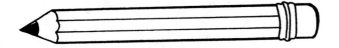

Color the pen blue.

Color the glue red.

Color the desk brown.

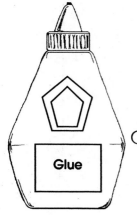

Color the stapler green.

My School Wordsearch

```
B  L  A  C  K  B  O  A  R  D
I  C  R  A  Y  O  N  S  G  T
N  H  C  L  P  E  N  C  I  L
D  A  S  C  I  S  S  O  R  S
E  L  U  U  D  E  S  K  N  P
R  K  G  L  O  B  E  U  H  A
T  S  T  A  P  L  E  R  U  P
A  E  B  T  E  L  G  L  U  E
P  U  C  O  M  P  U  T  E  R
E  M  A  R  K  E  R  P  Y  I
```

BINDER	COMPUTER	GLUE	PENCIL
BLACKBOARD	CRAYONS	MARKER	SCISSORS
CALCULATOR	DESK	PAPER	STAPLER
CHALK	GLOBE	PEN	TAPE

My School

My school is _____

My classroom _____

Grade _____
Room # _____
Teacher _____

My School

This is me at school.

This is my schoolyard.

Clothing
Introduction to Activities

Duplicate, cut out and mount the individual clothing pictures found in Visual Aids, pages 62-64. Play oral matching games with them.

"Clothing Bingo" cards are provided on pages 40-43. Use these for additional practice of the target vocabulary.

After adequate oral practice has been done, complete page 44 with the student. Read each word aloud and see if the student can find the correct picture. He/she will draw a line to connect the word to the picture. Ask the student daily, "What are you wearing today?.

The student should independently complete the self-portrait on page 45. He/she may rely on the individual clothing picture cards for the correct spelling of each item of clothing shown in the self-portrait.

With the ESL student, look around the room. Take turns secretly choosing a classmate and describe his/her clothing, i.e. "He is wearing green pants, a yellow shirt and black shoes. Who is he?" Students will enjoy this guessing game and benefit from the oral practice when they feel confident enough to give the clues.

Read picture books which utilize clothing vocabulary. There are some listed in the bibliography on page 7.

Use page 46 to review color and clothing words.

Page 47 provides additional reinforcement of body and clothing words. Initially, you may need to demonstrate the question and possible answers to assist comprehension of the assignment.

Clothing Bingo

Clothing Bingo

Clothing Bingo

Clothing Bingo

Clothing

Draw a line to connect the picture with the correct word.

pants

dress

shoes

hat

shirt

coat

shorts

boot

Clothing

Draw a picture of yourself.

I am wearing a _____

_____

_____

_____

_____

Clothing

Color the boy's shirt **green**.
Color the boy's shoes **black**.
Color the boy's pants **blue**.
Color the girl's shoes **red**.
Color the girl's hair **brown**.
Color the girl's pants **blue**.
Color the girl's shirt **yellow**.

Clothing

Circle the correct answer.

Where do I wear my . . . . ?

1. Where do I wear my pants?   foot   hand   leg   head

2. Where do I wear my hat?   foot   hand   leg   head

3. Where do I wear my shoe?   foot   hand   leg   head

4. Where do I wear my sock?   foot   hand   leg   head

5. Where do I wear my mitten?   foot   hand   leg   head

6. Where do I wear my boot?   foot   hand   leg   head

7. Where do I wear my glove?   foot   hand   leg   head

8. Where do I wear my cap?   foot   hand   leg   head

9. Where do I wear my highheel?   foot   hand   leg   head

10. Where do I wear my shorts?   foot   hand   leg   head

SSR1-12

Weather

Introduction to Activities

Duplicate, cut out and mount the individual weather pictures, found in Visual Aids, pages 69-71. Use them for oral matching games.

"Weather Bingo" cards are provided on pages 49-52 for additional practice of the target vocabulary. The four seasons are illustrated by a tree, with different foliage and/or experiencing precipitation specific to a season.

A blank calendar, found on page 53 has been included. Use it for daily practice. Ask the student what the weather is like each day and have him/her draw a simple symbol such as a sun or raindrop to illustrate the weather. At the end of the month, you may wish to count together to discover how many days the weather was sunny, cloudy or rainy.

Use page 54 to practice the names of the seasons and some common weather words.

Use page 55 to review clothing vocabulary and decide what clothing will be appropriate for each season. Read the completed sentences aloud with the student. This will serve as a planning sheet for the next activity.

A student booklet is provded on pages 56-57. The student should illustrate each page with a self-portrait showing clothing appropriate for that season. He/she should complete the sentence by writing the names of the different articles of clothing. A personal cover page for the booklet may also be assigned.

The final page in this section, page 58 should be completed by the student. Using pictures from magazines, discuss favorite activities and sports and have him/her categorize them by season. He/she may list or illustrate them in the appropriate box.

Weather Bingo

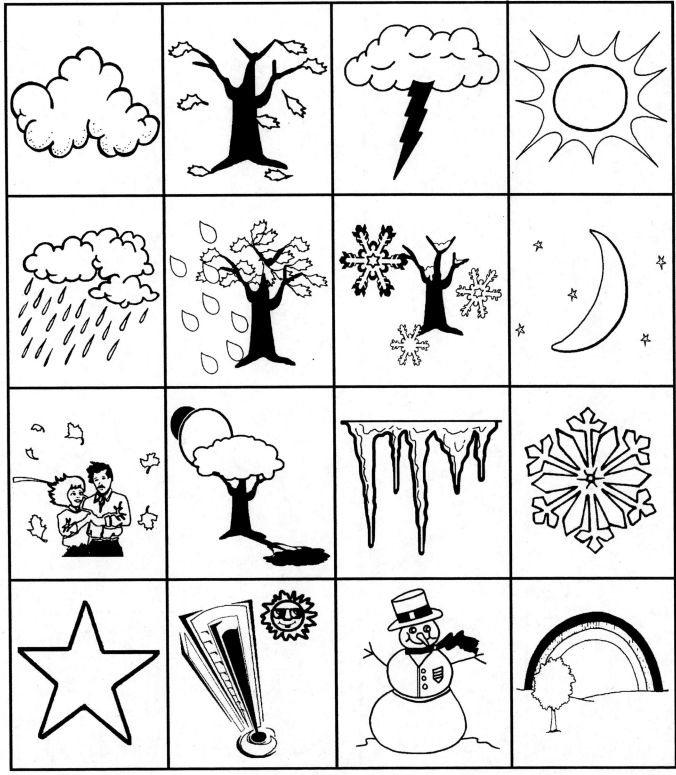

Weather Bingo

Weather Bingo

Weather Bingo

Weather

Month:						
Saturday						
Friday						
Thursday						
Wednesday						
Tuesday						
Monday						
Sunday						

SSR1-12

Weather

Use words from the wordbank to fill in the blanks.

lightning	summer	sun
hot	windy	fall
rain	spring	winter

_____

_____

_____

Weather

shirt	mittens	socks	sweater
hat	boots	cap	gloves
highheels	dress	shorts	coat
jacket	t-shirt	pants	shoes

On a cold **winter** day I wear

_____ _____

_____ _____

_____ _____

_____ _____

On a windy **fall** day I wear

_____ _____

_____ _____

_____ _____

_____ _____

On a wet **spring** day I wear

_____ _____

_____ _____

_____ _____

_____ _____

On a hot **summer** day I wear

_____ _____

_____ _____

_____ _____

_____ _____

Weather

In **spring** I wear _____
_____
_____
_____

In **summer** I wear _____
_____
_____
_____

Weather

In **fall** I wear _____
_____
_____
_____

In **winter** I wear _____
_____
_____
_____

Weather

Things I do in spring	Things I do in summer
Things I do in fall	**Things I do in winter**

Visual Aids

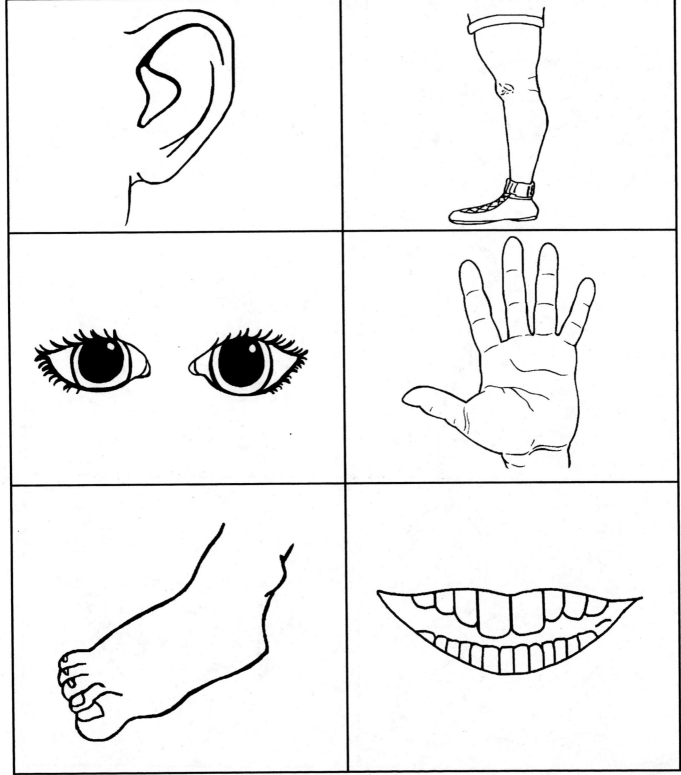

Visual Aids

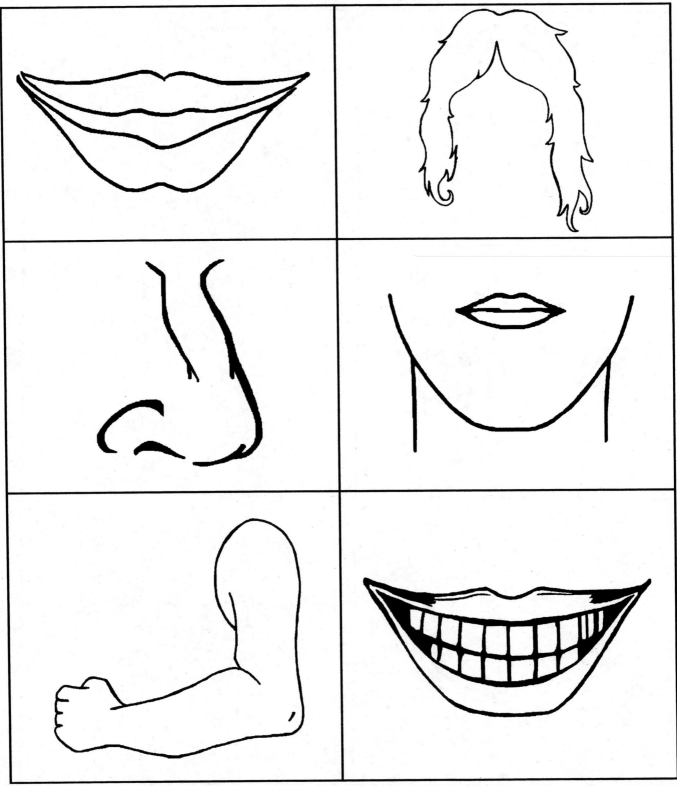

Visual Aids

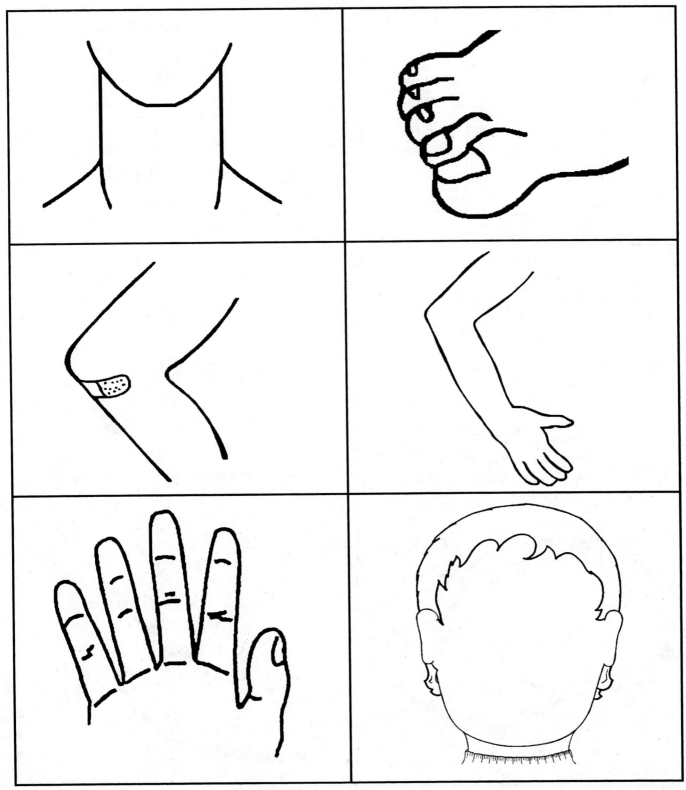

Visual Aids

Visual Aids

Visual Aids

Visual Aids

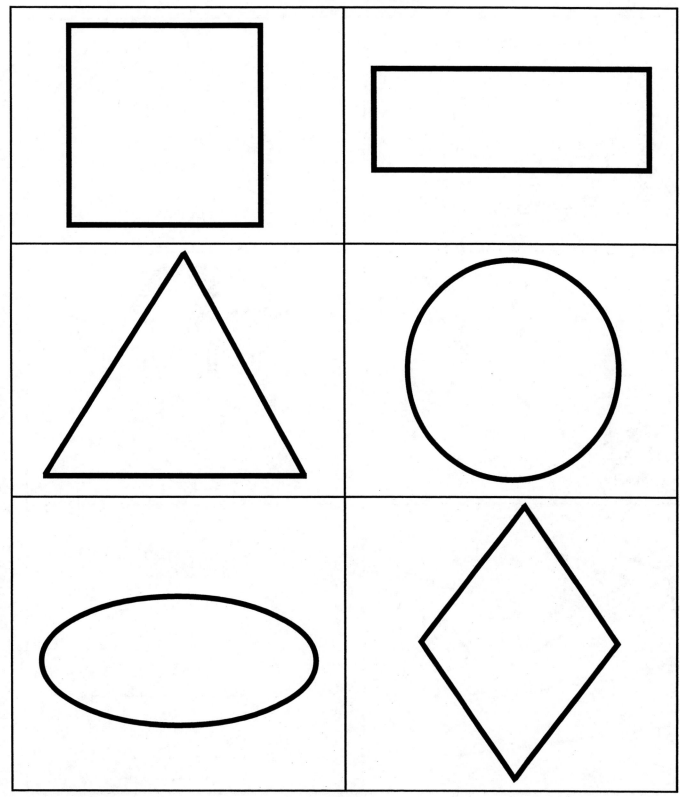

Visual Aids

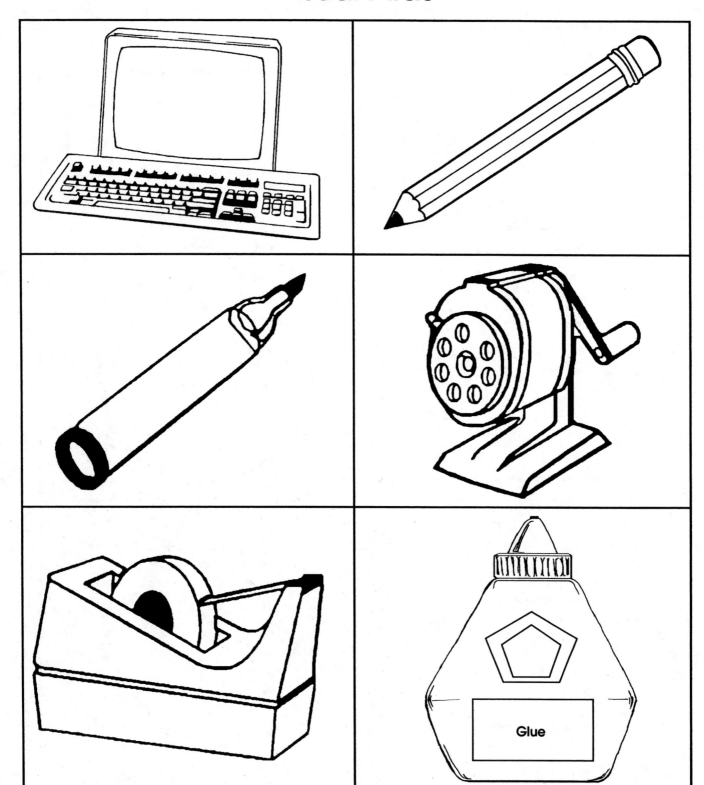

Glue

SSR1-12

Visual Aids

Visual Aids

Visual Aids

Visual Aids

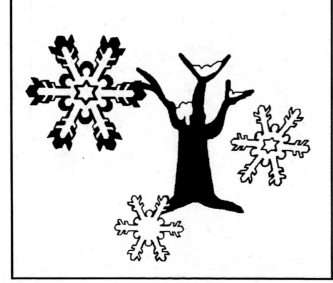 

Visual Aids

 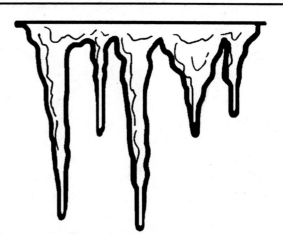

SSR1-12

Visual Aids

Tic/Tac/Toe

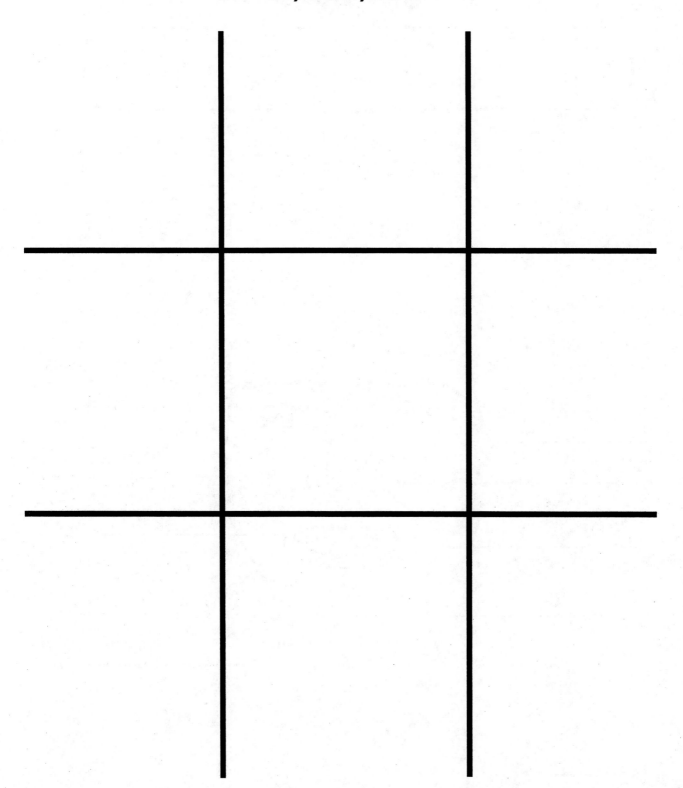

73

Getting To Know Me

nose	mouth	ear	eye	eyebrow
cheek	chin	hair	teeth	neck

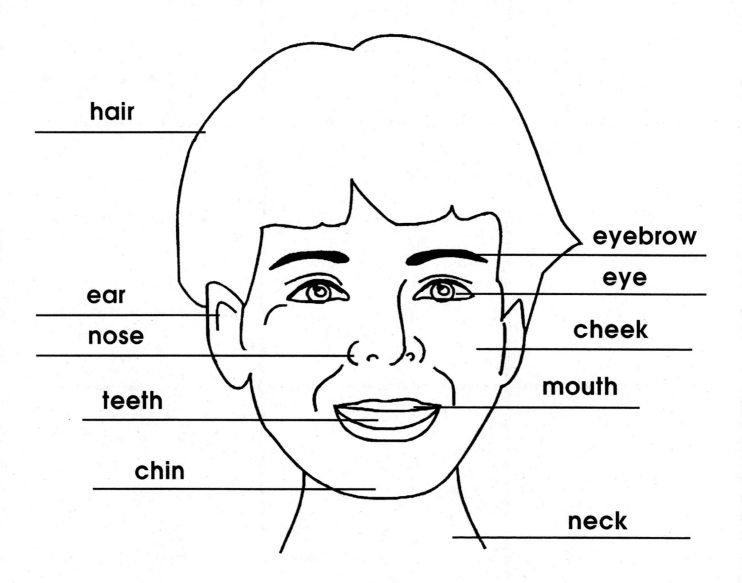

hair

eyebrow

eye

ear

cheek

nose

mouth

teeth

chin

neck

Getting To Know Me

leg	hand	arm	foot	neck
face	elbow	toes	fingers	hair

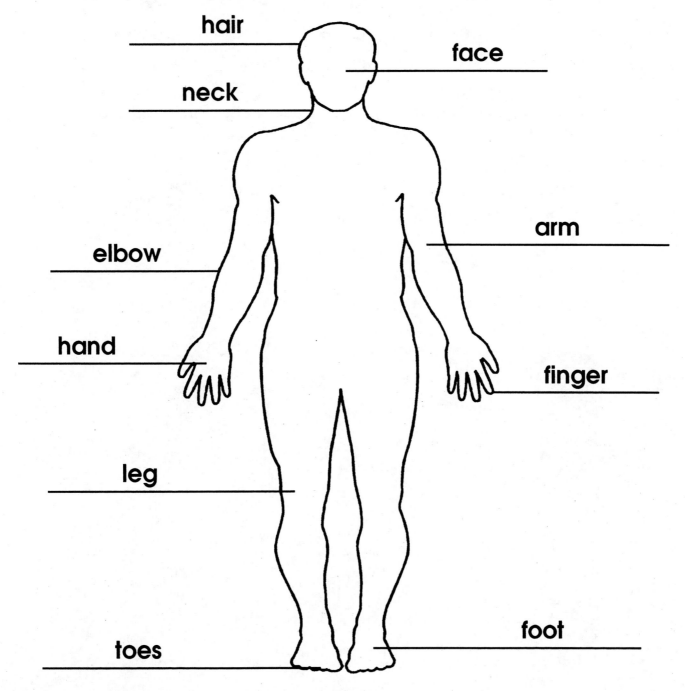

hair

face

neck

arm

elbow

hand

finger

leg

foot

toes

Getting To Know Me

Where do I belong?

cheek	foot	ear	chin	hand
mouth	toes	elbow	hair	eyebrow
nose	neck	eye	arm	teeth
	fingers		leg	

Head	*Face*	*Body*
hair	eyebrow	foot
ear	eye	toes
	cheek	neck
	mouth	elbow
	chin	arm
	teeth	hand
	nose	fingers
		leg

My School Wordsearch

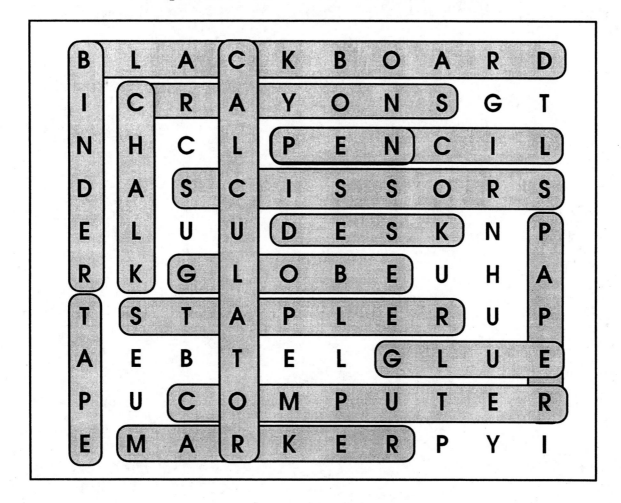

BINDER	COMPUTER	GLUE	PENCIL
BLACKBOARD	CRAYONS	MARKER	SCISSORS
CALCULATOR	DESK	PAPER	STAPLER
CHALK	GLOBE	PEN	TAPE

Weather

Use words from the wordbank to fill in the blanks.

lightning	summer	sun
hot	windy	fall
rain	spring	winter

summer

fall

lightning

sun

hot

windy

rain

spring

winter

SSR1-12

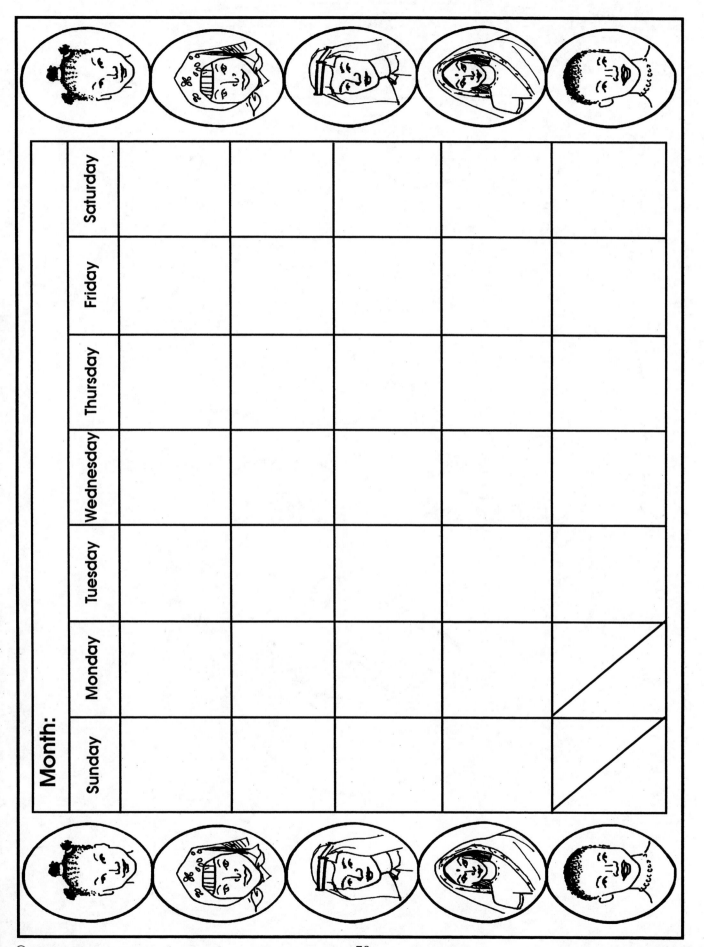

Month:

Sunday	Monday	Tuesday	Wednesday	Thursday	Friday	Saturday

SSR1-12